As I See It

a new book for all lovers of poetry

by

Eleanor G. Dix

THE AUTHOR

My early life was spent in East Retford, Nottinghamshire, where I was employed as a professional photographer's assistant.

I married a Norfolk man, whom I had met years earlier when he was evacuated in 1943 to Retford, and I now life in Halvergate, Norfolk.

I enjoy painting and gardening.

First published in Great Britain by The Dix Press, Halvergate, 2003
©E. G. Dix, 2003
ISBN 0-9545653-0-4

To order copies of this book, please contact the author on:
01493 700020

CONTENTS

CONTENTS

CONTENTS

CONTENTS

Beautiful Memories

Make beautiful memories.
Life may be short, life may be long.
Make of your life a beautiful song.

Your life is your own,
to give and to keep.
The love that you give, and
the love that you keep.

From your birth to your dying,
happiness supplying,
all memories complying.

Think back on pleasure,
of work and of leisure.
And may it remain,
again, and again, and again.

That Certain Look

Without a single word, I knew
that love did signal, I love you.
This power overall, so still,
does conquer all to fulfil.
A meeting in the eyes that portrays
a look, that all other looks erase.
So time will tell, if love will reap
a harvest, and that love to keep.

In the Summertime

Life is like a flower that grows.
In Summertime it's beauty shows.
When Autumn petals fall around,
like human beings upon the ground,
we find, too late, all are as one.
So short a time, then we are gone.

Life

Fold away your dreams
into the dream time drawer.
Take out your waking thoughts,
and open wide the door.

Feel the breath of morning,
awaken to the day.
Dance to the tune of the piper
until it fades away.

Today

Sitting on a fence, legs swinging, toes twirling,
stones hurling,
a boy lazing alone.
Here is magic, this fence his throne.
His mind is full of dreams,
or so it seems.
Above, the blue sky, where kites fly,
where other dreamers play, fields away.
And magic alone surrounds.
There are no bounds today.

Waiting

Silently is the prayer, inwardly the hope.
Each second, seemingly to share
a thousand memories of yesteryear.
Minute can be the noise
which makes the pulse race faster,
to be shattered as the noise decreases.

Eternity demands these things of mortal man,
knowing the universal secret.

Where is a joy without a sorrow,
where is hope without tomorrow?

Party Piece

I met him at an office dance.
He said that his name was Lance.
I found out later this was a lie,
He was the usual kind of guy.
He talked a lot about himself.
Proposed, then left me on the shelf.

Young and Beautiful

She really was bewitching
and made a great impression.
Her eyes so green, her neck so white,
she really was a wondrous sight.
So slim, so sleek, so very meek.
She only stayed for one whole week
and then we learned she lived next door,
with kittens, one, two, three and four.

Rosy Tinted Spectacles

I see what I want to see.
I believe what I want to see.
My Mind is intoxicated.
The world is my oyster,
I find out, after many pairs of glasses,
Men are just the same,
and so are Lasses.

5

A New Breed

I wander through a night of dreams,
or so it seems,
and I awake to see the sun.
To know that I can make a start,
of how I wish the day to go,
and hope that life, for me, will be
not too far from tranquillity.

But should it be that things go wrong,
life is so short, though days seem long.
So make the best of life for others.
We all are someone's children,
daughters, sons or brothers.
In this world someone will care
for those who secretly despair.

Reality

Where the bridge spans over the river's flow,
as it sparkles in the sunset's glow,
reeds bend at the water's edge
with the bullrush, iris and the sedge.

The swallow skimming as she darts in flight,
to catch some midge or fly in sight.

Cool green fields and shady trees,
brown and orange woodland bees.

Tree bark, moth and dragonfly,
and the first star in the evening sky.

Little Mouse

Dew is for bathing.
Sun is for warmth.
Corn is for eating.
Ears are for listening.
Nose is for searching,
in the soft earth.

Whose Fault is It?

The world is full of all,
I began, I crawled,
I toddled, I walked, I ran.

Work followed school,
or so I thought,
but life offered nought.

I am a man who tried
to follow life's pattern.
So, follow me, feel free
to watch TV.
To smoke, take drugs —
Who cares for me or thee?

Take me back to whence I came.
Come back after death?
Are you insane!

Ballad of Man

When the long night has gone
and the weeping turns to song.
When the East has met the West,
with nuclear weapons, germs, unrest.
Shall another peace begin?
Who will lose and who will win?

Let each man, who has a cause
in his heart, gently pause.
And, in his contemplating, seek
all that is in him that is not weak.
For Man, within him, holds the key,
and makes within him his own destiny.

The Poppy and The Cross

Where are the flowers that blossomed and grew,
where are the trees that once I knew?

Gone are the paths I used to tread,
where is the fly on the spiders web?

Black is the earth, and acrid the fumes,
where once was beauty, is now entombed.

Both sides have fallen, and are risen again,
upon this charred battle field,
where death ends all pain.

A Thought

If I should die before the dawn,
put on my grave a sheaf of corn,
so that the birds will have a feed
and I will have done my last good deed.

War

Do not count me in
if you wish to sin,
to maim and kill.
Do not count me in.
Why kill the reason for living?
Be forgiving.

Do not kill another you,
be they Arab or Jew,
Black or white, brown or yellow,
just another type of fellow.

Born to live, born to die.
Why, oh why, dear God, why?
Do not count me in
if you wish to sin.

Fight of Giants

Mother! Hear me! Hold me tight
from the terrors day and night.
From the bombs and shells that fall,
hear me mother, when I call.

Mother, which way shall we go,
who is our friend, and who is our foe?
East and West, it is all the same,
bombs and shells, they have no name.

Awake my mother, see the sun,
another bloody day begun.
Mother, Mother, look at me,
lifeless now, triumphant, free.

Gypsies in Winter

Whither shall we wander? By the cat iced fen,
on the heathland, where the heather dies to flower again?

Whither shall we camp now? On some grassy bank
by the river, deep dark river, cold and dank?

Modern cars have we, our caravans are new,
but where friendships count, friends are far and few.

Whither shall we wander? Whither shall we go?
Shall we find a little space, a little haven too?

Only for a little while, we travellers on the road,
Wish, like you, to find some peaceful abode.

A Problem for Thinkers

Am I a fool to be content with nought,
to sit and watch the world go by?
Am I a fool the world has wrought,
to look from out and then to sigh?

Can I solve the problem of black and white,
or take the care from aged folk?
Can I help to put them right,
or is it all just one big joke?
Is the life, which we are given,
worth the tears, and worth the joys?
Is there hell and is there heaven?
Or just solar explosions which creates and destroys.

Space

Space is like a child at play,
all forgotten — gone away.
Unto the world of composed thought,
every dream can be sought.
Children with imagination
join thoughts with every nation.

Love, Have You a Dream to Share?

Love, have you a dream to share
of love in time of suffering?
Where separation makes a longing,
and love is time stretched.

Love, have you an answer to a prayer
where only thoughts can satisfy
the loneliness and longing,
the heart break and the singing?

Time is a drug which all must take
to make each little world complete,
until the pain has vanished,
and in the silence of the mind give thanks.

September Song

I stand at the brink of eternity,
my hands stretched out in time.
The memory blossoms and fades,
and is reborn again.

How many times shall I hear,
how many times the pain?
Each new time I remember,
and come back to you again.

Sweet Innocence

A crown of daisies adorns her head.
Sweet innocence, alone she walks
beneath the branches, bending low.
Full blossomed white, the thorn,
carpeting the lawn below.

The years pass, yet still she walks
beneath the leafy thorn.
In spirit only.
She may pass once more
this sunlit morn.

In Appreciation

In twilight's declining years;
youth passed by,
nought the same;
never again.
Of deed, kindly done,
in gentle spirit,
an aged heart has won.

The Maker of Dreams

I sell dreams, for I am the maker of dreams.
I sell dreams to match each purse.
A billion for he who has all, but cannot sleep.
Special dreams for children,
who have secrets to keep.

Buy a dream time ticket. Buy one, buy two.
On the wings of night, do as others do.
Magic is my mission, let me make a dream for you.
Buy a dream time ticket,
only one euro.

Dreams

I saw a woman in a crowded street,
dancing so prettily, with sandalled feet.
Twirling and stepping so delicately,
set my heart dancing, and I followed her.

Through the alleys tripping,
through the town so fair.
Up the green clad mountains,
in the scented air.

On and on we travelled
by the waterfall.
And then she vanished from my sight,
I never saw her more.

A Feeling

There is a look that time defies,
a look, expression in the eyes.
No one knows from whence it came,
It has no definition, it has no name,
and no one has ever solved the mystery,
or ever will throughout history.

As it Used to Be

The briars grew thick, and the wild rose bloomed.
The skylark sang his song.
The humming bees passed over head,
and I could only sit and dream.
For here I knew nought could go wrong.

A Walk in the Countryside

Green, brown, and blue —
the colours of a sleepy summer's day,
when blackbirds sit upon the hawthorn bough and sing,
and fallen blossoms drift away.

Cool, beneath the clustered branches
of the tall and stately trees,
carpets of moss, as soft as velvet, steal,
and gently humming is the sound
of honey gathering woodland bees.

The silver gliding stream,
with ripple round from pebble tossed.
Time to wander, time to think.
To nature now my heart is lost.

A Second Spring

I saw a honey bee in a fine November mist.
An autumn day, when the sun the earth had kissed.
Before the winter's snow upon the earth was seen,
a second spring appeared and turned the earth to green.

A robin, hopping lightly, in a slightly rakish mood,
and dragging from the earth, a wriggling worm for food.
Spring flowers border flower beds upon this November day,
Oh, hold eternity still and let the second spring stay.

Oslo Basin

Oslo sleeps,
while a jewelled crown adorns her head.
The sky, with an incandescent glow,
selects colours from the spectrum,
scattering them upon
the black ridged flow.

October Sea

Soft blanket clouds of grey and blue.
Brown coloured sea.
Sand a yellow hue.
White topped gentle breakers,
lapping pebbles on the sand,
twixt sea and land.

Exile

When you think of me, my love,
when you think of me.
Catch the falling blossoms
from the apple tree.
When I think of thee, my love,
when I think of thee.
Let our hearts united be,
loving and sincere.

Cold Beauty

I walk alone and no one hears my cry.
I walk alone along the wind swept shore.
I sigh for you, I cry for you.
Listen to me just one more time.

Do you hear me call your name
in an empty room?
Through the portals of the night
I sigh for you. I cry for you.
My love, listen to me just one more time.

When first we met upon this shore,
our eyes met in loves first dance.
Our hearts beat like the surging tide.
Listen to me just one more time.

Now I walk alone upon this shore
only time is by my side.
Only white horses ride —
you are no longer by my side.

First Love

I had a love, oh! such a love.
We met each eventide;
I held his hand and, lovingly, we walked
side by side.

Each loving kiss I treasured dear,
and thought our love would never end.
Ah! sad the day. I thought my heart would break
never more to mend.

Three days I traversed all alone.
I wept, and tears were strong.
How sad each second seemed,
and each day oh! so long.

The years have passed,
but the memories linger.
Here I remain. The years have flown,
love was lost, now gone.

Thoughts of Love

To love.
To be in love.
Know you which love it be?
For love of mankind, I do love thee.

To be in love with only one,
and when that love has gone?
ah! me
I did love thee,
I did love thee.

Loneliness

No one will know that I sighed.
No one will know that I cried.
No one will know that I tried.
No one will know that I lied.
No one will know that I died.
Only the ebb and flow of the tide.

Yesterday is Today

Love is a never ending dream.
Yet, I cannot sleep, cannot eat.
All I do is hope — hope for you —
love you.

Sweet memories possess me,
how you caressed me.
Never forget, all we meant to each other
cannot destroy sweet separation.
No time arresting,
only a blessing, never ending.

Norway

In every tree my heart is singing.
In every tree I live.
My heart is in the crystal rock.
My love is in the moss that grows,
beside the deepest wild red rose.

Skagerrak

Black satin sea at early dawn,
with smoothed folds of softest silk.
Resplendent in the mystic morn,
the tresses of the night are gone.

New day arise, and stretch you arms
with laden brushes paint the skies.
All Heaven awaits you —
Aurora with the laughing eyes.

Earth, Sea and Sky

The sea calls and I answer back
"The land holds me!
I am for the earth beneath my feet."
The wind calls in the tree tops.

Drifting foam bubbles, caressing the pebbles
ridge by ridge,
pools hollowed out by wind swept waves,
edged by shelly sand, glisten in intermittent sunlight.

Marram, on risen dunes, stands sentinel,
building fortresses, as if to bait the oncoming tide.
The earth calls me and I answer back
"The sea calls me."
I am for the sea and the sky.
The sea breezes caress my face.

I long to hear the splash of waves,
to feel wet sand beneath my feet,
to dream of nothing more than this reality.
Earth, sea, and sky are my tranquillity.

Break of Day

Wild white plum blossom,
blowing across the lawn,
as the sun breaks through,
heralding the dawn.
Every bird with fluted voice,
seems to say rejoice, rejoice.
A new day is born.

Before Traffic

Upon the marsh five swans sat;
A pen, a cob and cygnets three.
And by the marsh road, a sparrow hawk,
with glinting eye, sat silently upon a tree.

Sheep and cattle grazed alone.
Gulls and lapwing pecked around,
and the wind in the reeds was the only sound,
except for my footsteps upon the ground.

The Storm

The rain splashes on the window pane.
The wind howls it's song, again and again.
No bird stirs.
The trees flay around to the music of the storm,
drilling, drum like, upon the mud splashed lawn.

Curtain of the Night

The moon the orb of night,
with incandescent light,
defeats the clouds of grey and black,
and lights the curtain of the night.

Trees sway, each tormented by the angry air,
that goes upon its wayward flight,
upon the curtain of the night.

No calm to interpose,
no ease for living thing,
or shelter man or mouse
in field or road.
No silence in the house.

The Unreality of Reality

The moonlight turns the landing
into a quiet world full of imagination.
Corners, unnoticed before, reveal
a hidden intensity of what might be.
And the area of shadows
opens up a new reality.

Void

I sit and look into the fire,
as if the world were taking shape.
Each little crevice between the coals
depicts an ever moving scene.
As crumbling ash breaks momentary vision,
and all that little world is rent asunder.

Genesis Exodus

Who can remember?
Who has not suffered?
Untold emotions sweep through the mind.
I am alone.
Yesterday's thoughts intrude into daily routine,
who am I? What am I?
A genetic interpretation since the beginning of man,
a human jigsaw, with the last piece missing.

Your Church, Your Choice

Empty stone churches,
empty stone hearts.
No time existing for even a thought.
How are we living,
just money existing?
No more ideals, before we depart.

Not Lost

There is always hope.
Love lost, love to gain.
There is always hope.
Yesterday's love, memories to heal,
Memories to remain.
In this world of sorrows,
there is always hope.
And in the end, hope will remain,
love to gain.

Their Heaven, Our Hell

Should we be sad or happy
when someone we loved has died?
Tears there were, and we cried, we cried.

Remembering happy times,
and now that their pain has ended.
Their memory will be tended,
and in our hearts never forgotten.
The years will ease our pain
yet, still in our hearts, forever remain.

Rain

The clouds are weeping for the world,
hiding away the sun.

The spring is mourning
daily, natures work is done.

The day's eyes open, birds sing;
but the heart of the season has but a dull ring.

Oh! Phebos Apollo look down from the skies,
and send your smile down on the earth and her cries.

Compassion

Oh! Let in the sun, the window bars are not a prison.
Outside the sparrow, with her faith in nature,
flies or hops in search of food
for her journey through another day.

Let us take note of how each creature,
which we do not call human,
performs its daily tasks,
and then we might recall
how mechanical we could become
without them.

A Blessing

This is October in the year of our Lord
Nineteen Hundred and Sixty-Eight.
The Summer sun is still afire
as if to Autumn no desire.
Although the flowers, trees, and fern
are mid, betwixt the two.
The blending of the seasons ekes out one's little life,
and pleasant is the solitude,
'neath skies of blue and white.

At Peace

The singing quiet sleeps within my waking,
gentle, as birds in flight
over oceans waves, in nature breaking.

Floating fantasies of clouds drift in summer skies,
as petals of the pear tree fall,
and I am thoughtful in this solitude, and wise.

Ulvik

Silver topped mountain against the dark fir,
wind through the tree tops makes the branches stir.

Gulls dive over the fjord, calling as they go,
waterfall cascading, high the mountain snow.

Green sweeping reaches, topped with pine,
air as cold as Christmas, but as sweet as wine.

35

Threads of Life

The ribbons on the maypole are my memories.
They thread and intertwine,
no sequence evident.
The sunlight dapples the branches of the trees,
and interweaves, tinting the clustering leaves.

In far off fields once trod by children's feet,
memories stir,
daisy laden chains — adorning heads.

The ribbons twirl upon the maypole's sturdy post,
and lads and lasses, clasping hands,
laughing, dancing into eternity.
The ribbon red within my outstretched hand I lift above my head.
And through the mist I see Summers past.

Lost Love

Lay gently down in that sweet sleep of death.
Here, seemingly, ending the earthly phase.
Life, so dear, so short, in stillness ends.
Youth, once more in countenance, attends.

Well remembered of her yesteryears,
in beauty grace and gentle manner.
Missed by many, blessed on earth.
May peace attend for her new birth.

Tryst

Will you walk down the lane with me
and sit beneath the old oak tree,
whisper sweet nothings in my ear
and call me darling, love and dear?

Will you hold my hand,
and loving go down to the meadow,
where buttercups grow,
and pick for me a golden crown,
before we hurry back to town?

What is Love?

What is love?
Giving birth,
holding the hand of a child?
This is love!

What is love?
Is it the passion of two beating hearts?
This is love!

What is love?
Caring for all,
selfless devotion?
This is love!

What is love?
Love is love,
nothing destroys.
This is love!

Time to Dream

Child of mine close your eyes,
dream time is full of surprise.
Sleep until the sun breaks through,
may the journey last long for you.
And when you awake,
another journey you will make.
Until dream time comes once more,
and you go through the dreamland door.

Innocence

Do you know why she runs away?
Like children all who go to play,
life is full,
life is new.
Happiness in her little heart rings,
she does not know what tomorrow brings.

No Need for Words

There are no words but singing birds,
there is no day but yesterday.
The sweetest flower that blooms will fade,
there is no love but in the heart.

In the East of Iceland

In the fields, by the dusty roads,
grow dandelions supreme, huge and verdant green,
and bobbing heads of cotton grass
blow kisses into the air, white and fair.

Across ditches, mud filled, wire stretched,
horses graze, long flowing manes.
And eyes that gaze, and gaze.
The air is still.
Traffic is for visitors upon the quiet dusty road
where once I strolled.

Love Song

You came to me,
our love was new,
new as the spring time,
after the winter's snow.

Let our hearts say
all the things that lovers say.
I cannot bear the pain of parting
at the end of each day.

Love is all we have,
there is no need for words.
Let the music of each day
be for singing birds.

In Air

We are but dreamers, you and I.
In thought, we wander hand in hand.
By sighing willows in the wind,
by murmuring streams, meandering along,
drifting and dreaming life's eternal song.

Look! Look to the east,
where the patterned sky shows its first beauty.
Shafts of sunlight from the door of heaven streams
and perpetuates our inward dreams.

We are to the open air to wing our thoughts.
Too solid the ground beneath our feet.
Boundless ideals are lifted up, and swept away.
Our apple orchard is full.

Song

I give my heart
to you, my love.
I give you all,
I give you love.
Why don't you care?
Care! Care for me.
Life is lonely, so lonely.

When you are away
each lonely day,
I pray awhile.
The minutes stay.

Come back to me,
I need you so.
My life is empty
without you.

In Love

Clear light of dawn,
when beauty springs from slumbering night
and birds sing of morning in joyous flight.
Yet, no more, abundant life is glad,
and, awakening, throws open her arms
to embrace the day, and night is forsaken.

Silence

If the whole world took a vow of silence,
how quiet it would be.
To listen to the wild things,
to listen to the sea.

Then reason could take over
and reason might prevail.
But, how would we impart this knowledge?
Ah! that is another tale.

Question

The smile on your face
brings a smile to mine.
What were you thinking
in that inkling?

Before forty
I have noticed you for quite a while.
Why have you that enigmatic smile?

Perhaps, one day, I will find out
what it was all about.
And having found the reason why,
blush, and feel extremely shy.

That Tantalising Look

Who knows the secrets of another's heart?
A look, a smile may beguile.
But will that look of innocence, or passion,
keep in fashion, or depart?

45

Too Big Your Hat

How many writers have there been
with knowledge to impart?
How much notice do we take,
or do we make the same mistake?
Think we know all there is to know?
It only goes to show,
that, throughout all history,
life is still a mystery.

Knowing

I know, you know, we know,
everyone knows.
We are born. We live, we die.
With this we all agree.
But in between, who knows
why we disagree?

Searching

So much to do, so short a time.
The being and the world is mine —
the earth the stars the universe.

Too great a God, to perfect follow.
The soul alas is cold and shallow —
where is the love of fellow man?

I am at the beginning of a new ideal.
Teach me humility and to feel —
teach me to love.

A Crush

Oh love! You make me tremble,
from the top of my head to my toes.
Oh love! Should you smile at me,
red cheeks I then would show.
Oh love! My heart's a patter.
Alas, you do not know.
But if you should learn to love me,
I would never let you go.

Basically We Never Change

Basically we never change
but as time passes rearrange.

Maiden of the Earth and Skies

Spring is the curtain which floats over Winter's rest,
and every colour, delicate, as fresh as morning dew.
Sultry days of Summer, with deepening greens and blues.
She trips over fields and meadow,
with gossamer light shoes.

Her tresses are of yellow, with streaks of burning gold,
and interlaced with ribbons of red and purple hues.

She wears her gown of turquoise,
of brown, and grey, and white,
and sheds her tears, like pearl drops,
where earth and sky unite.

Robin

Sitting on a brown oak tree, a robin sang
trilling notes of ecstacy.
The sun, now warm at noontide gleamed,
and then his vivid feathers preened.
Was ever song so sweetly sung?
His little heart with praises rung.

The Ladybird

It came and sat upon my hand,
a pretty, pretty thing.
It was the colour of a flame,
with coal black spots upon it's back.
And then it flew away with open wing.

Pastoral

Come daylight with the dawn,
your fingers stretched across the sky,
each with its pastel hue,
to show what life can hold anew.

Opening the locked embrace,
kindling yet the eternity,
speeding the light away.

Into the velvet dusk
unfolded night has come,
away, away 'tis done, 'tis done.

Crescendo

Am I an intruder into this verdant domain of lofty trees
and mountain terrain?
Of tumbling waters, over grey green rocks,
and deep gorges, and mountain tracks?
Ages of man, with the earth's buried wealth,
competing with nature in courage and strength.

Morning Noon and Night

The day breaks and the sleeping bird awakes.
Morning is stepping into light,
as day puts on her raiment,
and folds away the night.

The hour is still, as if an unknown will,
portrayed how each sunlight hour should be.
The singing bird is resting in the tallest tree.

The setting sun slowly sleeps,
and evening light, with vivid colours
streaked across the sky,
before the purple night descends
and ends the Summer's day.

Man Alone

Deep, dark, the clouds, sentinel stationed
above the silhouetted roof tops,
where lighted window panes
throw patches of artificial sunshine
upon the pebbled forecourt.

Distant humming tells of traffic in city streets.
Here, modern torches, in varied styles,
help the motorist to speed along.
And journeys end, in great percentage,
before the television screen.
To sit around, each, in his little world,
quite willing to see, but be unseen.

Dreaming 1996

My age is on the outside,
My ego is within.
I cannot see myself,
but your heart I hope to win.
Although too old for romancing,
friendship means a lot to me.
You set my heart dancing.
You set my spirit free.

Wishing

I send to you, my love.
I send to you the light.
I send to you all happiness.
I send to you the night.

All things which bring you pleasure.
All things which dispel pain.
I send to you the sunshine.
I send to you the rain.

To you my heart is given.
But my name I may not unfold.
Or you may think I am teasing.
Or very, very bold.

True Love

Shall I tell you what true love is?
Do you really wish to learn?
To find someone who agrees with
every thought you hold most dear?

Love is something we are given
and partake each waking day.
Love is in the song of wild birds
as the dawn begins to break.

Love is gentleness and caring,
when all others turn away.
Captured moments in eternity,
which quickly seem to fly away.

True love is philosophical.
One gives, and hopes for love returned.
Love is, in the end, forgiving,
when one is once again spurned.

Lullaby for Children of All Ages

A silver orb on a sea of blue and black,
wuther the wind around the chimney stack.
The singing kettle at supper time,
joins in chorus with the grandfather clock's chime.
The dog is asleep on your favourite chair,
and a creak is heard from every stair.

Listen. Oh! listen to the music of the night,
and you will sleep so soundly,
with your eyes shut tight.

Fire in the Sky

Winter sunset, all aglow,
Throws streaks of red upon the snow,
And lights the tree bark's mistletoe.
There feeds the thrush with speckled attire,
next to the blackbird on the briar.
Then sinks the sun to night of whitened snow,
and the full moon's incandescent glow.

Summer Solitude

Do not look up to the light.
The day's eye is opened wide and white.

Upon the shore of golden sand
which stretches twixt sea and land.

I wander in a carefree mood,
and all that glories in me,
in this pure solitude.

Let the breezes blow through my hair,
as I go down to the sea.

Today I am happy, today I am free.
The stones are washed by the waters,
that eddy and swell,
and the murmurings of the sea, many stories could tell.

That Little Black Dress

I have that little black dress
    but I have nowhere to go.
I must confess,
    it is cut a little too low.
I take it out of the wardrobe
    and try it on, once in a while.
It is a little too tight on the hips,
    and quite out of style.
But the memory of younger days
    gives me a thrill,
as I take my bedtime drink
    with a sleeping pill!

Does It?

Do you do as others do?
Should you do as others do?
Does it matter if others do?
They are they, and you are you.
Do they know what you do?
Do you know what they do?
Does it matter what you do?